semillitas
de aprendizaje™

Semillitas de aprendizaje is a series of bilingual (Spanish/English) children books by the Intercultural Development Research Association that is based on the **art of storytelling**. These culturally-relevant stories are for children to listen, view and then read along. The children eventually begin to repeat the stories and learn the art of creating their own stories as well as recite poetry.

Semillitas de aprendizaje **stems from research** IDRA has conducted on its Reading Early for Academic Development (READ) project, funded by the U.S. Department of Education, to establish in preschool centers "classrooms of excellence" that ensure **reading, cognitive and emotional success** for all preschool children through a print-rich environment with appropriate accommodations for children with disabilities.

This storybook is available both as a bilingual big book (abridged) and as this smaller bilingual storybook (unabridged).

◇◇

IDRA is an independent, private non-profit organization, led by María Robledo Montecel, Ph.D., and dedicated to assuring educational opportunity for every child. As a vanguard leadership development and research team for more than three decades, IDRA has worked with people to create self-renewing schools that value and empower all children, families and communities. IDRA conducts research and development activities, creates, implements and administers innovative education programs and provides teacher, administrator, and parent training and technical assistance.

"Children need places that are safe, that are nurturing, that welcome their families, that welcome their culture and their language and have them really be able to learn and prepare themselves for life. There is a saying I like: 'See yourself in the eyes of a child, see yourself in hope.'"

– Dr. María "Cuca" Robledo Montecel, IDRA President & CEO

MANAGING EDITOR AND LEAD AUTHOR
Abelardo Villarreal, Ph.D., IDRA

CONTRIBUTING AUTHORS
Oralia H. Lamas
Rosana Rodriguez, Ph.D., IDRA

ILLUSTRATOR
Thelma Muraida

EARLY EDUCATION READING CONSULTANTS
María Elena (Mari) Riojas Lester, M.E.
Sylvia R. Manzano, M.A.
José L. Rodríguez, M.A., IDRA
Dr. Bradley Scott, IDRA

ENGLISH LANGUAGE EDITOR
Christie Goodman, APR

Jesusita y las Arañas / Jesusita and the Spiders (unabridged storybook)
Semillitas de aprendizaje

Questions and requests for permission will be most generously handled by: Intercultural Development Research Association; 5815 Callaghan Road, Suite 101; San Antonio, Texas 78228; Ph. 210-444-1710; Fax 210-444-1714; E-mail: contact@idra.org; www.idra.org

ISBN 978-1-935737-08-7

Distributed by the Intercultural Development Research Association. Manufactured in the United States.

This document was prepared in part with funds provided by the U.S. Department of Education and the W.K. Kellogg Foundation. The opinions expressed herein do not necessarily reflect the position or policy of the U.S. Department of Education or the W.K. Kellogg Foundation and no endorsement should be inferred.

INTERCULTURAL DEVELOPMENT RESEARCH ASSOCIATION
María "Cuca" Robledo Montecel, Ph.D., President & CEO
5815 Callaghan Road, Suite 101
San Antonio, Texas 78228
210.444.1710 • fax 210.444.1714
CONTACT@IDRA.ORG • WWW.IDRA.ORG

Jesusita y las Arañas

Desarrollado por Intercultural Development Research Association

Jesusita le tenía miedo a las arañas. Cuando las veía, corría despavorida. Un día ella vio una araña colgada del techo de la cocina.

—¡Qué horror! —gritó Jesusita, mientras corría por el patio de su casa. Sin fijarse, se tropezó con Carmen, su hermana mayor.

Al verla tan agitada, Carmen le preguntó,
–¿Qué pasa que vienes gritando?
–¡Vi algo que parecía un insecto colgado del techo de la cocina!
–respondió Jesusita.

A Carmen le preocupó mucho que Jesusita estuviera tan asustada.
—Vamos a averiguar qué viste colgado del techo —le dijo Carmen
a Jesusita. Y juntas se dirigieron nuevamente a la cocina.

5

—¿Dónde viste ese animalito? –preguntó Carmen.– ¡Hay que ver si es insecto!"

—En ese rincón –dijo Jesusita, apuntanto al techo de la cocina.

—Es sólo una pequeña telaraña —exclamó Carmen.
—Y lo que cuelga de la telaraña, ¿es un insecto que
me puede picar? —preguntó Jesusita temblando.
—Es una arañita. No es un insecto. Y tampoco es una araña
venenosa. Es una arañita indefensa —respondió Carmen.

Muy cuidadosamente, Carmen metió la arañita en un frasco.
Las dos muy atentas observaron que la arañita parecía
perdida. —Busca cómo salir del frasco —gritó Jesusita.
—Pobrecita, no te lastimaremos. Sólo te tendremos aquí por
un ratito para observarte y estudiarte —le dijo Carmen a la
arañita.

—Toma el frasco, hermanita. No te pasará nada. Esta arañita no es venenosa y es muy bonita —le aseguró Carmen a Jesusita.
—¿Cómo sabes eso? —preguntó Jesusita.— ¿Cómo puedes distinguir las que son venenosas?

–Es muy fácil –le explicó Carmen.– Lo leí en un libro de la biblioteca.
Las venenosas son brillosas. Hay dos clases de arañas que son muy
venenosas. Ésas son la viuda negra y la araña solitaria marrón.
También aprendí que hay arañas que nos ayudan.
Algunas comen muchos insectos que son dañinos a las personas.

—Entonces, ¿las arañas no son insectos? —preguntó curiosa Jesusita.
—En realidad, las arañas no son insectos. Los insectos tienen alas,
antenas y seis patas. Las arañas no tienen alas ni antenas. Tienen
ocho patas —explicó Carmen.

12

—Los animales de ocho patas se llaman arácnidos —añadió
Carmen.— Hoy hemos aprendido mucho acerca de las arañas.

Desde ese día, Jesusita comprendió que es muy bueno estudiar e
investigar a los animales vivos en vez de tenerles miedo. También
descubrió que su hermana y los libros podrían ayudarla siempre.
Ya Carmen no va sola a la biblioteca. ¡Ahora Jesusita va con ella!

From that day on, Jesusita understood that it is good to investigate and learn about living things instead of being afraid of them. She also found out that her sister will always help her and that books can teach her many things. Now, Carmen doesn't go to the library by herself. Jesusita goes with her!

"Animals with eight legs are called arachnids," added Carmen.
"We have learned a lot about spiders."

"So, aren't spiders insects?" asked Jesusita, curious.
"In fact, spiders are really not insects. Insects have wings, antennas and six legs. Spiders do not have wings or antennas. They have eight legs," explained Carmen.

"That's easy," Carmen explained. "I read about it in a library book. I also learned that some spiders are very helpful. Some eat many insects that are harmful to people." "The poisonous ones are shiny. There are two types that are very poisonous. They are the black widow spider and the brown recluse spider," Carmen added.

Intercultural Development Research Association

Carmen said kindly. "You hold the jar, little sister.
Nothing is going to happen. This is not a poisonous
spider, and see how pretty it is."
"How do you know that?" Jesusita asked. "How can
you tell which ones are poisonous?"

Very carefully, Carmen put the little spider into a glass jar.
Both girls observed how the spider seemed lost. "It is looking
for a way to escape." Carmen said, "Poor thing, we won't
hurt you. We will only keep you here for a little time so we
can look at you," Carmen explained to the spider.

Carmen exclaimed gently. "It's only a small spider web."
"But what's in the web, won't it bite me?" asked Jesusita trembling.
"It's not an insect. It's a spider. And it's not a poisonous spider. It's only a
harmless little spider," replied Carmen.

"Show me, where did you see the insect?" asked Carmen. "Let's see if it's really an insect."
"There it is!" said Jesusita pointing to the kitchen ceiling.

"It's probably just a spider, Jesusita. Let's find out exactly what
you saw hanging from the ceiling," says Carmen.
The girls walked together to the kitchen.

Seeing that she was so excited, Carmen asked, "What's the matter, Jesusita? Why are you screaming?"

"I saw something that looked like an insect hanging from our kitchen ceiling" replied Jesusita out of breath.

"Oh my goodness!" she cried and she ran through the house to the patio. Without watching where she was going, she bumped into her older sister, Carmen.

Jesusita was afraid of spiders. Every time she saw one, she ran away as fast as she could go. One day she saw a spider hanging from the kitchen ceiling.

Jesusita and the Spiders

Developed by the Intercultural Development Research Association

"Children need places that are safe, that are nurturing, that welcome their families, that welcome their culture and their language and have them really be able to learn and prepare themselves for life. There is a saying I like: 'See yourself in the eyes of a child, see yourself in hope.'"

– Dr. María "Cuca" Robledo Montecel, IDRA President & CEO

Managing Editor and Lead Author
Abelardo Villarreal, Ph.D., IDRA

Contributing Authors
Oralia H. Lamas
Rosana Rodriguez, Ph.D., IDRA

Illustrator
Thelma Muraida

Early Education Reading Consultants
María Elena (Mari) Riojas Lester, M.E.
Sylvia R. Manzano, M.A.
José L. Rodríguez, M.A., IDRA
Dr. Bradley Scott, IDRA

English Language Editor
Christie Goodman, APR

Jesusita y las Arañas / Jesusita and the Spiders (unabridged storybook)
Semillitas de aprendizaje

This document was prepared in part with funds provided by the U.S. Department of Education and the W.K. Kellogg Foundation. The opinions expressed herein do not necessarily reflect the position or policy of the U.S. Department of Education or the W.K. Kellogg Foundation and no endorsement should be inferred.

INTERCULTURAL DEVELOPMENT RESEARCH ASSOCIATION
María "Cuca" Robledo Montecel, Ph.D., President & CEO
5815 Callaghan Road, Suite 101
San Antonio, Texas 78228
210.444.1710 • Fax 210.444.1714
CONTACT@IDRA.ORG • WWW.IDRA.ORG

semillitas
de aprendizaje™

Semillitas de aprendizaje is a series of bilingual (Spanish/English) children books by the Intercultural Development Research Association that is based on the **art of storytelling**. These culturally-relevant stories are for children to listen, view and then read along. The children eventually begin to repeat the stories and learn the art of creating their own stories as well as recite poetry.

Semillitas de aprendizaje **stems from research** IDRA has conducted on its Reading Early for Academic Development (READ) project, funded by the U.S. Department of Education, to establish in preschool centers "classrooms of excellence" that ensure **reading, cognitive and emotional success** for all preschool children through a print-rich environment with appropriate accommodations for children with disabilities.

This storybook is available both as a bilingual big book (abridged) and as this smaller bilingual storybook (unabridged).

◇◇◇◇◇◇◇◇◇◇◇◇◇◇◇◇◇◇◇◇◇◇◇◇◇◇◇◇◇◇◇◇◇◇

IDRA is an independent, private non-profit organization, led by María Robledo Montecel, Ph.D., and dedicated to assuring educational opportunity for every child. As a vanguard leadership development and research team for more than three decades, IDRA has worked with people to create self-renewing schools that value and empower all children, families and communities. IDRA conducts research and development activities, creates, implements and administers innovative education programs and provides teacher, administrator, and parent training and technical assistance.